ISBN: 0-8010-2332-7

Library of Congress Catalog Number: 72-94218

Copyright 1968, 1972 by Baker Book House Company

Fourteenth Printing, January 1977

Printed in the United States of America

TO

the cherished memory
of my grandparents
Mr. & Mrs. O. W. McDonald

and

Dr. Elizabeth Williams
Dean Emeritus of Southern Bible College

and

All My Former Students
who have experienced the thrill
of "moving the tassel"

acknowledgments

Judi Treat
Peggy Branscum
Nellie Gabbard
Shizuka Kasai
Donald A. Bass
Mamie Caldwell
Terri L. Caldwell
Louis R. Caldwell
David A. Caldwell
Paul B. Caldwell

contents

Trust in the Lord with all thine heart;
  and lean not unto thine own understanding.
In all thine ways acknowledge Him,
  and He shall direct thy paths.

— Proverbs 3:5, 6

1

that bittersweet moment

"What kind of book would you appreciate at the time of graduation from high school?"

This was the question I asked high school seniors before preparing this book. To get different points of view, I went to college freshmen and asked them to look back and, in the light of their experiences since graduation, tell me what they would like to have included in a book such as this. Many of the replies were very helpful. Here are a few of the typical ones:

> How to be a success
> How to choose a college
> How to choose a career
> How to make decisions regarding marriage and the
>   draft
> How to enter the future with confidence
> How to know God's will for my life

Not only were the seniors quite sure of the kind of information they wanted, but they also had definite ideas as to the way in which it should be presented. "Please don't overstress the solemn facts, responsibilities, obligations, and pressures that face us," they pleaded. "It's not that we don't want to face up to our future, but if the picture is painted too black, we're apt to think that the challenge is too great." Another common request was, "Let us know what's ahead. Be realistic without being preachy."

However, these questions and concerns have not been the only guidelines for writing this volume. More than anything else I wish to share a deep conviction that the high school graduate should be aware of Christ's presence, promises, power, and claims. Every youth wearing the cap and gown who recognizes his need of divine guidance, and who seeks earnestly to know and realize God's will for his life, can be assured of having the living Christ actively enter into his life!

Granted, there are more than three million youth who will graduate this year. But you are not lost in the crowd, not to the One of whom it was written: "He knew all men" (John 2:24b).

You are not only known to Him, you are also valued by Him:

> Are not five sparrows sold for two farthings, and not one of them is forgotten before God?
> But even the very hairs of your head are all numbered. Fear not therefore: Ye are of more value than many sparrows."
>
> — Luke 12:6, 7

Christ knows you as an individual and is aware of what your graduation means to you.

Remember how it was? You heard your name called and suddenly the moment had come. Your parents, teachers, friends, and fellow classmates watched as you strode across the platform to receive your diploma. Amid the camera flashes and applause you shook hands with your principal and accepted the symbol of having satisfactorily completed the equivalent of twelve years of formal classroom education.

As you walked off the platform your next act was deeply meaningful. You took your tassel and moved it over to the left-hand side of your cap. A new milestone in your life had been reached and you knew that feeling, that bittersweet feeling, that mixes the joys and successful struggles of the past with the question marks and challenges of the future.

A gifted young lady looked back from graduation and traced with insight and sensitivity the development of an important realization: "It was one day during the last few weeks of school," she began, "that I first saw her. I was on my way to the library when out of nowhere she came roller-skating down the cracked sidewalk. As I paused to let her go by, memories of my childhood came surging back — a rubbertire swing, long silk hair ribbons, cotton candy and taffy. Childhood was such a magic time.

"The next day I saw her again. She was standing across the street when school let out. After that I saw her every day, sometimes more than once a day.

She had long brown-gold curls and wore a pretty little dress which seemed strangely familiar. I never saw her face very clearly — it was always in the shadows. Who was she? Why did I see her so often? I tried to approach her, but when I came near she would run away. She would always come back though, and wait somewhere in the shadows. But as graduation drew near, I had little time to wonder about that silent child who waited — for what, I didn't know.

"Commencement night came at last, with its excitement and tension, and a touch of sadness. All day long I had been rushing about, trying to keep out the memories of those past years and the friends I'd be leaving. As I went out of the house something seemed to be missing. I realized I hadn't seen the child all day, and suddenly I felt very lonely.

"The evening passed swiftly. As we turned into the aisle to march out, I looked through the crowd, searching. There she was, sitting by my parents. As she looked at me I saw her face for the first time. In that brief moment I realized who she was and why she was there. An overwhelming sadness passed over me. This was the crossroads; she had come to say goodby."

Concluding her remarks, Mary said, "Perhaps, I would see her again, somewhere in the far distance: but it would never again be as it once had been. Our eighteen years together were ending. I had to go without her. As I went through the door, I took one last look. She was gone. I knew she would be."

Yes, Mary knew and so do you.

A nostalgic look at those wonderful "green years" blends itself with the realization that your achievement represents the combined efforts of a great many people. You were able to move the tassel and to receive the cherished diploma because of the sacrifices and dedication of parents, teachers, counselors — everyone who contributed to your life, many of whom you will never know. Perhaps the most deeply moving of all these realizations is that of having had the unseen help of Him whose assistance has been given you in a thousand wonderful ways.

All this and much more was yours at graduation. As the memories linger, you can savor with deep understanding the meaning of this Scriptural insight: "The desire accomplished is sweet to the soul" (Proverbs 13:19a).

2

"where to now"

Looking back at graduation, a young lady recalled ". . . this is the way it was: a time of joy, then the stirrings of doubt . . . goodbye to friends, some forever . . . memory of all the good things, the warm feelings of belonging . . . search for knowledge revealing frightening new lands . . . and now . . . where to now?"

Recall how it built up? Maybe it began with receiving your "senior" ring — how proud of it you were! Your high school yearbook finally came off the press and you began collecting as many signatures of classmates and teachers as possible. Then you were mailing your invitations and ordering your cap and gown. Applications to colleges and universities or for employment were being filled out, and replies were anxiously anticipated. Final exams were ahead, and the tension mounted.

Now that you have made it, you are in the company of thousands of others who stand with diplomas in hand, asking the question, ". . . and now . . . where to now . . . ?"

The Bible records the famous words of the wisest man in the world of his day: "To every thing there is a season, and a time to every purpose under the heaven" (Ecclesiastes 3:1). Now, at graduation, is the "time and the season" for deciding which direction your life will take and how you will prepare for what looms ahead.

A story is told about a sailor who was shipwrecked on one of the South Sea Islands. The natives found him, lifted him to their shoulders and carried him into their village. Little hope was held by the sailor as he imagined himself being served "well-done" to the natives that night at dinner.

His worries were replaced by astonishment, however, when they placed him on a throne and put a crown on his head. He was then proclaimed their king. The natives became his servants; his every wish was their command. For a while the sailor took full advantage of his new kingly status. But as time passed he began to wonder about it all.

Discreetly he questioned a few of the natives, and what he discovered came as a jolt. It seemed that each year the natives practiced a custom of making some man a king. He "reigned" one year, at the end of which time he was banished to an island and left there to starve to death.

Immediately the sailor began to ponder the future! He was a clever, resourceful fellow and soon came up with a brilliant solution. "Since I am still king," he reasoned, "the natives are still my servants. First, I'll have them build some boats. After they've done that, I'll have them take fruit trees to the islands where they plan to send me. There they can transplant the fruit trees, build some nice houses, clear some land and plant crops."

The commands were given and obeyed. At the end of his year as king, the natives were true to their custom. Only this time the banished "king" did not starve to death, thanks to his wise planning ahead!

What is the wisest way to plan for your future? Consider these two suggestions: (1) know where the rocks are and (2) prepare for life's inevitable experiences.

"My interest is in the future," said Charles F. Kittering, "because I am going to spend the rest of my life there." An interest in the future is important but more is needed: courage and direction are also essential. Facing the uncertainty of the future you find yourself identified with those who belonged to the Hebrew nation of long ago that camped on the brink of the Promised Land. There the Israelites received encouraging words from their new leader, Joshua. The words he spoke were given ". . . that ye may know the way by which ye must go: for ye have not passed this way heretofore" (Joshua 3:4).

How modern and meaningful are these words! "For ye have not passed this way heretofore." How can you know the way? "After the tassel is moved," how do you know which step to take next?

Three fishermen were anchored about a football field's distance off shore enjoying very little cooperation from the fun wearing scales and fins. One of the anglers decided that he would go ashore. He stepped over the side and walked across the water to the beach. No sooner had his feet touched the sand when another of the men announced that he too would go ashore. As the third man looked on with astonishment, his buddy duplicated the performance of the first man.

"Well," thought the man who remained in the boat, "if they can do it, so can I." And over the side he went — and straight to the bottom he plunged. He came splashing back to the surface and climbed back into the boat. But he was not one to give up too quickly Again he tried but with the same results.

The two men standing on the shore had been observing the futile efforts of their friend and were so weak from laughter they could hardly stand. Finally one managed to say to the other, "He'll drown himself if we don't hurry and tell him where the rocks are!"

Your future's surface covers the "rocks," the principles of a meaningful, effective, creative life. You do not have to have 20/20 vision to observe how often the rocks are missed. Conformity to conduct codes of today are not reliable supports or guides; cultural standards are a tide that changes and washes away faulty foundations.

Ann Landers, whose column is read by thousands of youth, knows where the "rocks" are. She wrote: "The answer to every problem can be found between the covers of the Bible." The great Christian educator, Dr. William Lyon Phelps, who was professor of English at Yale for many years used to tell his students, "I would rather have a knowledge of the Bible without a college education than a college education without a knowledge of the Bible." My own conviction as a former teacher of secondary-school youth and presently as Chairman of the Division of General Education and counselor at Southern Bible College is that as you stand at your new stage in life, the Bible is your best source of help. The eternal promises and principles found in God's Word will safely guide you into your future. They will chart a course approved by God. The Creator of the terrain is best qualified to give reliable directions and the Divine Mapmaker has done His part in pointing out "where the rocks are."

So certain is Jesus Christ about the results of living life His way that He ends the greatest sermon ever taught with these words:

Therefore whosoever heareth these sayings of mine, and doeth them, I will liken him unto a wise man, which built his house upon a rock:

*And the rain descended, and the floods came, and
the winds blew, and beat upon that house; and it fell
not: for it was founded upon a rock.*

*And every one that heareth these sayings of mine,
and doeth them not, shall be likened unto a foolish
man, which built his house upon the sand:*

*And the rain descended, and the floods came, and
the winds blew, and beat upon that house; and it fell:
and great was the fall of it.*

*And it came to pass, when Jesus had ended these
sayings, the people were astonished at his doctrine:*

*For he taught as one having authority, and not as
the scribes.*

— Matthew 7:24-29

To those who question the authority of His words
Jesus says, "My doctrine is not mine, but his that
sent me. If any man will do his will, he shall know
of the doctrine, whether it be of God, or whether I
speak of myself" (John 7:16b, 17).

Following the directions of the inspired Scriptures
you can be secure in the knowledge that when you
take the next step into your future you will feel a
rock underfoot!

The second principle of successful planning is
that of preparing for life's inevitable experiences.

Long ago there lived a man named Saint Philip
Neri, whose ability to teach law was known far and
wide. Eager young students would travel great dis-
tances to receive his instruction. He had an entrance
exam that he gave each new student.

"Why did you come?" he would begin.

"To study law," was the standard reply.

"What will you do when you have studied law?"

21

"I will set up my practice."

"And after that?"

"I will get married and have a family."

"What then?"

"I will enjoy my home and my work."

"Then what?"

"Then I will grow older and eventually die."

"And after death what then?"

Thus the great teacher would lead the student to the most certain of life's experiences — ". . . it is appointed unto men once to die, but after this the judgment" (Hebrews 9:27). Saint Philip knew that until the student was ready to die, he could not truly be ready to live. Alexander Dumas put it like this: "If the end be well, all is well."

The happiest, most effective life is lived by those who recognize life's "common ventures," such as death, work, marriage, and parenthood and prepare adequately for them. The Chinese have a proverb for it: "Dig your well before you get thirsty." The Bible has an example for it: ". . . the ant . . . which having no guide, overseer or ruler, provideth her meat in the summer, and gathereth her food in the harvest" (Proverbs 6:6-8).

How unlike the ant who looks ahead is the lightning bug, about whose frustration an insightful poet wrote whimsically:

> *The lightning bug's plight is a tragic one*
> *It's been said again and again.*
> *For he cannot see where he's going;*
> *He can only see where he's been!*

Looking ahead to the future and wondering which direction to take, you can plan with the greatest confidence, if like the psalmist you have learned: "Thy Word is a lamp unto my feet and a light unto my path" (Psalm 119:105).

3

"a sheath
without a sword"

In his poem "The Statue and the Bust," Browning describes a brilliant, talented young aristocrat as "a sheath without a sword." The youth was living a life without purpose. What good is a sheath, regardless of its potential and external attractiveness, and what good is life if it is without a worthwhile purpose?

Jane (not her real name) was a "sheath without a sword." Having graduated from a metropolitan high school with a perfect 5.0 average, she was the valedictorian of her class. She accepted a scholarship from a well-known university, and all who knew her were positive of her success.

In the process of enrolling, Jane suffered an emotional breakdown and was advised by a college counselor to return home. After returning home, she attempted to enroll in a large university in her hometown. Again the breakdown occurred. She consulted a doctor, and his examination revealed no organic excuse for her problem. A third time she attempted to enroll in college. This time it was a small junior college, and again she lost control.

Needless to say, Jane was in a state of despair. A few days passed and she came to my home to talk about her future. She related how that in junior high school she was denied an award that she felt she had deserved. In her opinion the award was given on the basis of personality. She was determined to prevent that from happening again. She decided to excel academically and drove herself to reach that goal. All her ambition and energy were directed toward reaching that objective. She reasoned that academic honors could not be denied her on the basis of personality. However, when her goal was reached, she discovered that she had nothing definite to look forward to. Lacking a strong enough purpose to continue, Jane found herself emotionally unable to enter college that semester.

Goals make the difference between the drifter and the doer. As someone said, "No wind is favorable if the captain does not know to which port he is steering." Goals give purpose to living. Lacking this purpose, many of today's college-age youth are unable to meet successfully the challenge and struggles of life. For some the frustration and despair becomes so great that suicide seems to be the only answer.

How tragic that any youth should despair of life and come to feel the same as Shakespeare's Hamlet, who cried:

O God! God!
How weary, stale, flat and unprofitable
Seem to be all the uses of this world!
Fie on it! Ah fie! 'Tis an unweeded garden,
That grows to seed.
— Hamlet, Act 1, Scene 2

A university student visiting Mexico discovered that the communist workers there were gripped by their goal of seeing the hammer and sickle over the entire world. He became a communist. Soon afterward he wrote a letter to his fiancee, breaking off their engagement. A Presbyterian minister obtained the letter and gave it to evangelist Billy Graham. Here is what the letter said:

We communists have a high casualty rate. We're the ones who get shot and hung and lynched and tarred and feathered and jailed and slandered and ridiculed and fired from our jobs. We are in every way made as uncomfortable as possible. A certain percentage of us get killed or imprisoned. We live in virtual poverty. We turn back to the Party every penny we make above what is absolutely necessary to keep us alive.

We communists don't have the time or the money for many movies, or concerts, or T-bone steaks, or decent homes and new cars. We've been described as fanatics. Our lives are dominated by one great over-

shadowing factor — the struggle for World Communism. We Communists have a philosophy of life which no amount of money could buy. We have a cause to fight for, a definite purpose in life. We subordinate our petty personal selves into a great movement of humanity, and if our personal lives seem hard, or our egos appear to suffer through subordination to the Party, then we are adequately compensated by the thought that each of us in his small way is contributing to something new and true and better for mankind.

There is one thing in which I am in dead earnest, and that is the communist cause. It is my life, my business, my religion, my hobby, my sweetheart, my wife and mistress, my bread and meat. I work at it in the daytime and dream of it at night. Its hold on me grows, not lessens, as time goes on. Therefore I cannot carry on a friendship, a love affair, or even a conversation, without relating to this force which both drives and guides my life. I evaluate people, books, ideas and action according to how they affect the communist cause and by their attitude toward it. I've already been in jail because of my ideas and, if necessary, I'm ready to go before a firing squad.

The Christian's goal is the same as that of the communist: world conquest! But there the similarity ends. Unlike the communist, the Christian has the advantage of knowing now who belongs to the winning side. "At the name of Jesus every knee should bow" (Philippians 2:10a). And again, "I am he that liveth, and was dead; And, behold, I am alive for evermore" (Revelation 1:18). The open tomb and the thrilling history of the Christian Church remind us of Him whose way of life lives on and will ultimately triumph!

A story is told of the time when a major oil company was looking for a representative to the Far East. Representatives of the firm approached a missionary and offered him $10,000. The offer was refused. They raised it to $50,000 and again he said no.

When they wanted to know his reason, he replied, "Your price is right, but your job is too small. God has called me to be a missionary."

What has God called *you* to be? You may not be certain of your *place* in life, but you can be certain that you have a *purpose* and that your life is important to God and to your fellowman. Albert Einstein said, "The man who regards his own life and that of his fellow creature as meaningless is not merely unfortunate but almost disqualified for life." Carlyle, the essayist, offers this insight: "The man without a purpose is like a ship without a rudder — a waif, a nothing, a no-man." He urges, "Have a purpose in life, and, having it, throw such strength of mind and muscle into your work as God has given you."

Some years ago Dr. Gansaulas, the famous Chicago preacher, was in his study writing a sermon when his nephew, a fine athlete in his early twenties, walked in. He noticed the text of his uncle's sermon: "For this cause I came into the world" (John 18: 37c).

"Uncle," said the youth, "I wish I knew why I was born." Dr. Gansaulas had known that his nephew had been having trouble finding himself. Now, however, he was given the opportunity to speak to the troubled young man when he was in a receptive mood. They talked about life for a while and the nephew left.

He had not walked far when he heard the sound of fire engines. The Old Iroquois Theater was on fire, eventually taking more than five hundred lives. When he arrived at the scene, the nephew noticed a number of people standing helplessly at a balcony window.

Picking up a heavy plank, he raced into the building next to the theater and laid the plank across to the window. Many people were saved by the bridge. During the rescue mission a piece of heavy timber tore loose, knocking the youth to the pavement below. His uncle reached him just before he died and said to him, "Now you know why you were born. You were born to save these people."

Later, Dr. Gansaulas was in Europe in a certain hotel. There he met a man in the hotel lobby and in the course of their conversation, the great minister mentioned that he was from Chicago. The other man suddenly became hysterical and began muttering something over and over. A man walked up and led his irrational friend away.

After a while the third man and Dr. Gansaulas were talking about the sad case. The man explained that his friend had been in Chicago one Saturday and went to the Old Iroquois Theater shortly before the great fire broke out. To escape the man climbed over many others who were panicking. He managed to get out unharmed but went crazy thinking about the experience. Over and over, he was heard to say, "I saved nobody but myself. I saved nobody but myself."

Great frontiers are yet before us. The West Coast youth who was asked about goals was wrong when he replied, "Goals? We've got no goals. Our parents have achieved them all for us." What about the physical frontier of space? the social frontier of freedom and brotherhood? the educational frontier of truth, knowledge and understanding? and above all, the spiritual frontier of the kingdom of God?

How many times have you said what is commonly known as the Lord's Prayer? Think again of the familiar words: "Thy kingdom come, Thy will be done on earth. . . ."

These are the words Christ taught us to pray. When we repeat them in our prayers we are making a wonderful and majestic plea: that His will and way of life cover the earth, that "man's inhumanity to man" cease, that peace and happiness reign everywhere, that sin and suffering be banished forever.

Whoever involves himself in cooperating with God in extending His kingdom finds the highest purpose for living that is possible. "The greatest use of life is to spend it for something that outlasts it," said William James. "But how," some may ask, "can I have a sense of individuality — find myself — if I live my life this way?" Christ Himself gives the answer to this dilemma:

For whosoever will save his life shall lose it; but

30

whosoever shall lose his life for my sake and the gospel's, the same shall save it.

— Mark 8:35

Everyone needs to be gripped by a deeply absorbing purpose that will give direction, power and meaning to his life. A meaningful life becomes possible when a person believes that his activities and relationships are directly and vitally connected to the goals he values. Ambition and responsible behavior result when these goals seem supremely worthwhile and attainable. For the Christian the goal of living his life to the glory of God is supremely worthwhile. Is this goal attainable? Get the answer yourself from the final words of the resurrected Christ as recorded in Matthew:

. . . All power is given unto me in heaven and in earth. Go ye therefore, and teach all nations, baptizing them in the name of the Father, and of the Son, and of the Holy Ghost: Teaching them to observe all things whatsoever I have commanded you: and, lo, I am with you alway, even unto the end of the world.

— Matthew 28:18-20

4

more important than a career

A certain high school graduating class chose for its motto this profound truth:

Your life is God's gift to you;
What you do with it is your gift to God.

Many Christian youth who have a deep concern regarding the will of God for their lives frequently ask, "How can I know what kind of work the Lord wants me to do?"

The best counsel at these times is probably this: Be certain that you are giving Christ a fully surrendered life. In obeying Him today you will be led into His will for you tomorrow. He can be trusted to guide you in choosing a life's work as surely as He can be trusted as Savior and Lord. Meanwhile, "Whatsoever ye do, do it heartily, as to the Lord, and not unto men" (Colossians 3:23).

Other suggestions for fulfilling your life's purpose would include (1) evaluating your interests and hobbies, (2) considering the courses in which you made the best grades, (3) talking to your high school counselor or a Christian educator and (4) reading books that explain qualifications of employees whose work has special appeal for you.

In the final analysis the important consideration is not the work but the worker. The reason why is dramatically illustrated in the ancient Greek tale of Achilles.

When Achilles was born his mother was told that her son had one of two destinies: he would either live a long, uneventful life of ease or a short life of glory and honor. Not wishing her son to die in his young manhood, Achilles's mother decided to hide him on an island. Nobody but girls lived on the island, so Achilles was dressed like a girl and was thought to be safely hid from harm.

Time passed and then there was war between the Greeks and the men of Troy. Finding themselves in danger of losing, the Greeks sought advice of the oracle as to how they might defeat their enemy. The oracle told them they must have the leadership of Achilles. Of course, no one knew where he was. A shrewd and cunning man named Ulysses was selected to begin the important search.

When at last he came to the island inhabited only

by girls, Ulysses disguised himself as a peddler. In his pack he carried beautiful ornaments and trinkets. Mixed with these were some gleaming weapons. True to their character the girls flocked around the gaily colored trinkets. Achilles found the attraction of the swords and shields irresistible. Acting true to his character he began brandishing the swords and fending off imaginary sword thrusts with the shields. When Ulysses saw that he cried, "Here he is, our hero, Achilles!" Being wise in the ways of men, Ulysses knew that *what a person chooses is determined by what he is.*

All talk about choosing a life's work does little good without stressing that *character is more important than a career.* You did not have to graduate in the top 10 percent of your class to be able to see how it works. You have heard the word *success* used in frequent conversations and speeches during the last few weeks. Few words can compete with *success* around graduation time, but what is the meaning of the word? Examine the following definitions:

> *The superior man makes the difficulty to be overcome his first interest; success comes only later.*
> — *Confucius*

> *The secret of success is constancy of purpose.*
> — *Disraeli*

> *If you wish to succeed in life, make perseverance your bosom friend, experience your wise counselor, caution your elder brother, and hope your guardian genius.*
> — *Joseph Addison*

34

Success lies not in achieving what you aim at, but in aiming at what you ought to achieve.

— Anonymous

Notice a point that each definition has in common with all the others: success is not a goal, but the result of developing and exercising qualities of character. In the final analysis success is not what we do, but what we are; not what our actions are, but what our attitudes are. Those who seem to have success did not seek after it, and those who make it their life's aim, seem never to hit the target.

"A man's life," said Jesus, "consisteth not in the abundance of things which he possesseth" (Luke 12: 15b). In the biography section of your school's library you could probably find a biography of David Livingstone, the famous missionary. Few people know that he had a brother, John, who became one of the wealthiest men in Ontario. Both boys grew up together in a Scottish home. Although John and David had the benefits of the same instruction, each set his heart on reaching different goals. John decided to gain wealth; David responded to the command of Christ: ". . . If any man will come after me, let him deny himself, and take up his cross, and follow me" (Matthew 16:24). John reached his goal and enjoyed a comfortable life of luxury. David reached his goal, too, and after giving his life to convert the heathen in Africa, he died there in a dirty little hut. But which brother had the richer life? When John died, his demise was reported in a few brief words in the obituary column. Ironically, the only distinction given him was that of identifying him as the brother of David Livingstone!

Rudyard Kipling once addressed a graduation class in Canada. In his speech, Kipling cautioned: "Don't put too much emphasis on fame and fortune. Some day you will meet a man who needs none of these things, and then you will know how poor you are."

Winston Churchill was reported to have asked an actress, "Would you marry a man for a million dollars?"

"Of course," she replied.

"For five hundred?"

"Of course *not!* What do you think I am?"

"We have already established that, my dear," said Churchill. "Now we are only trying to determine the degree."

Someone has pointed out that money will buy

A bed not but sleep
Books but not brains
Food but not appetite
Finery but not beauty
A house but not a home
Medicine but not health
Luxuries but not culture
Amusement but not happiness
A crucifix but not a Savior.

Christian youth must spare themselves the disillusionment that poisons life when love of money motivates the setting of life-goals and the investing of ability, time, and energy. Jesus was not unaware of our materialistic needs. He assured us their satisfaction if our values were properly focused. ". . . Seek ye first the kingdom of God, and his righteousness; and all these things shall be added unto you" (Matthew 6:33).

If fame and money bring success and happiness, why would a very famous playwright who had both confess, "I suffer great periods of depression." To attempt to lift himself out of his valleys of gloom, he relies mainly on drink and pills. "My intake of liquor," he reveals, "is about a fifth a day — half of a fifth of bourbon and half of a fifth of vodka." Added to that is the problem of insomnia. To get some sleep, says he, "I take up to four sleeping pills." Evidently the man who writes about life, has not learned to live it successfully. He admits, "My analyst helps me and without him I'd be sunk. I go to him five times a week."

How one wants to invest his life should be the top-ranking concern of every Christian graduate. Basically there are only two ways of investing your life: by getting all you can, or by giving all you can. The greatest authority on the good life advised us as to which way brings the greater rewards. He said, "It is more blessed to give than to receive."

Christian character must express itself through service. Your life's work should be governed by a passion to please Christ, determined by an unreserved surrender to His will, directed by your awareness of need and your ability to meet that need, and energized by the Holy Spirit's daily influence upon your dreams, preparation, associations and activities.

Horace Mann, called by many the Father of our American Public School System, once said, "Be ashamed to die until you have won some victory for humanity!" Now, while you stand at the colon of the sentence of your life, listen to the unknown poet's words:

> There is a voice within you calling,
>   To higher and better things.
> In constant yearning and great
>   Heart burning,
> A beautiful song it sings.
>   'Tis the voice of God
> In your Spirit Life,
>   In your most hidden spring;
> Who can know what you can be
>   And do as a man —
> That's the beautiful song it sings.

5

consider
the wilderness way

A drop-out at thirteen! She did it, she said, "to concentrate completely on my goal." Few thirteen-year-olds are that certain about their future. "Even then, I knew exactly what I wanted," she said. Her goal? To sing in opera.

To reach that coveted goal, Roberta Peters had to spend many hours in vocal studies. Three years passed and she was offered the leading role in a Broadway musical. The salary looked astronomical and the lure of Broadway danced before her eyes. But if she signed the contract, it would mean being away from her training for opera for a year or more.

Needing advice, sixteen-year-old Roberta went to her teacher. He counseled her this way: "You are good, Roberta, but you can be better. If you take this detour, you'll never know how far along the straight road you might have gone." She refused the short cut and four years later made her Metropolitan Opera debut in Mozart's *Don Giovanni.*

"I know what I want, and the sooner I can get it, the better I'll like it; and please don't ask me to wait!" This is the kind of attitude that develops "detour-takers."

Credit (or discredit) our present-day culture for its influence on strengthening the appeal of the shortcut. Ours has been called the push-button society. The emphasis is on speed and our "computer culture" makes it hard to develop patience. The "itch of the instantaneous" is a disease that is reaching epidemic proportions.

Remember the Red Queen in *Through the Looking-Glass?* Rushing through the Looking-Glass Wonderland with Alice in hand, she kept crying out all the time, "Faster! Faster! Don't try to talk. Faster!" Maybe the Red Queen is another name for our time. We might try to catch our breath long enough to ask if all this activity indicates achievement. You wonder if a certain pilot was speaking of us when in answer to a passenger's question, "How're we doing?" he replied, "We're lost, but we're making good time!"

When so many young people in this hurry-hurry-hurry age are rushing into marriage, taking shortcuts in education, and job preparation, it is uncommon to consider the counsel of Roberta Peter's teacher: "If you take this detour (or shortcut), you'll never know how far along the straight road you might have gone."

"The straight road" has no geometrical significance; rather, it means the best direction to take to reach a worthwhile goal. More often than not, "the straight road" looks like the "long way around."

One of the most remarkable journeys in history is found in the Book of Exodus. Led by the brilliant Moses, the nation of Israel journeyed from Egypt to Canaan, the Promised Land. Allowing twenty miles per day for the average walking time, they should have been able to reach their destination in ten days. How long did it take them? Forty years!

Why? ". . . God led the people about, through the way of the wilderness . . ." (Exodus 13:17, 18). What was the reason for this apparent waste of time? Dr. G. Campbell Morgan explains it: "God led them that they might learn the truth about themselves by that long discipline."

Life's most treasured gifts take time to possess. There is no shortcut to Christian character, personality, poise, skill, a trained mind and cultured maturity. These gifts cannot be hurried. How long, for example, does it take to develop the qualities described in Kipling's unforgettable lines:

If

If you can keep your head when all about you
Are losing theirs and blaming it on you.
If you can trust yourself when all men doubt you,

But make allowance for their doubting too;
If you can wait and not be tired by waiting,
    Or being lied about, don't deal in lies,
Or being hated, don't give way to hating,
    And yet don't look too good, nor talk too wise:

If you can dream — and not make dreams your master;
    If you can think — and not make thoughts your aim;
If you can meet with Triumph and Disaster
    And treat those two imposters just the same;
If you can bear to hear the truth you've spoken
    Twisted by knaves to make a trap for fools,
Or watch the things you gave your life to, broken,
    And stoop and build 'em up with worn-out tools:

If you can make one heap of all your winnings
    And risk it on one turn of pitch-and-toss,
And lose, and start again at your beginnings
    And never breathe a word about your loss;
If you can force your heart and nerve and sinew
    To serve your turn long after they are gone,
And so hold on when there is nothing in you
    Except the Will which says to them: "Hold on!"

If you can talk with crowds and keep your virtue,
    Or walk with Kings — nor lose the common touch,
If neither foes nor loving friends can hurt you,
    If all men count with you, but none too much;
If you can fill the unforgiving minute
    With sixty seconds' worth of distance run,
Yours is the Earth and everything that's in it,
    And — which is more — you'll be a Man, my son!

Despite our incredible scientific progress, there is still no coin-operated machine that, if you put a quarter in it, will produce twenty-five cents worth of wisdom, or any of the other treasured gifts! You have to go "by way of the wilderness" to be able to say:

I am young enough to have joys and sorrows, deep longings and high dreams, and many, many problems, but old enough to know there is a cause for every joy, a cure for every sorrow, a solution to every problem, and fulfillment for every aspiration.

I am young enough to desire success, but old enough to know it should never destroy health or character.

I am young enough to want money, but old enough to know that true wealth consists not in abundance of things one possesses.

I am young enough to covet fame, but old enough to know that better than fame is the joy of spending oneself in self-forgetful, loving service.

I am young enough to enjoy a good time, but old enough to know one cannot have a good time if pleasure-seeking is put first in life.

I am young enough to be enthusiastic over people and things, but old enough not to let any enthusiasm run away with me.

I am young enough to love to play, but old enough to have learned that most fun is having a hard task and seeing it courageously through.

I am young enough to want to be beautiful, but old enough to know true beauty comes from within.

I am young enough to seek far and wide for the Truth, but old enough to know that it is most often found in being faithful to the task in hand.

I am young enough to make many mistakes, but old enough to learn the lesson, forget the experience, and pass on to better things.

I am young enough to dread pain, sorrow, misfortune, but old enough to be grateful for their chastening, mellowing influence.

43

I am young enough to long for happiness, but old enough to know it tarries longest with us when we seek it least.

I am young enough to crave true friends, but old enough to appreciate them when I find them.

I am young enough to believe passionately in the goodness of the human heart, but old enough to keep that faith regardless of some disillusionment.

I am young enough to know the meaning of love, but old enough to realize it is life's most priceless possession.

I am young enough to have faith in God, in His goodness, in His loving care over me, in His wise and beautiful plan for my life, but old enough to value this faith as the thing that gives life purpose and makes it worth living.

Said George Henry Lewis:

Many a genius has been slow of growth.
Oaks that flourish for a thousand years
Do not spring up into beauty like a reed.

Those who rush through their period of preparation live to regret it, as the following letter to Abigail Van Buren shows:

Dear Abby: I have a problem that bothers me immensely. We have a new minister whose language is atrocious. I can hardly sit through his sermons anymore. He says, "He done," "had went" and "They is." Abby, don't you think that after four years in Bible college he should be able to do better than that? My ten-year-old son notices these mistakes and mentions them to me. Is there a remedy?

Small Town

*Dear Small: I don't know how "small" your town is,
but if the people were bigger they could raise enough
money to import a more literate minister.*

Abby could have added to her answer that the
minister might have gone through four years of college, but four years of college had not gone through
him! Of course grammatical speech is not a minister's most important asset; he should above all else
declare the "full counsel of God." But why can't this
be done with grammatical correctness? Talking to
his ministerial students over one hundred years ago,
C. H. Spurgeon said, "The time is past when un-
grammatical speech will suffice for a preacher." Like
all other abilities, the ability to speak correctly takes
time and effort to develop.

The "way of the wilderness" is another name for
being able to postpone satisfaction of some present
need to attain a more worthy goal in the future. This
requires a high degree of self-discipline, but the rewards make the effort worthwhile.

A full, useful life is the result of a great and wonderful unfolding process. As the Scriptures state,
". . . First the blade, then the ear, after that the full
corn in the ear" (Mark 4:28). Moreover, it is the
result of a cooperative endeavor between you and
your God. This truth is beautifully expressed in Bob
Benson's "Perspective." As you read it, you will be
reminded of the reward of "the wilderness way":

God and I raised a flower bed.
He really did the most
I guess.

45

We used
His soil,
His air,
His water,
His life,
His sun.
My part seemed so trivial that
I said,
"Lord, You take those bulbs and
make them grow
right there in the box
Out in the garage.
You don't need me, Lord,
You can do it by yourself."
"Oh, no," He said —
"I want to do My part;
I'm waiting to begin,
But you must do yours, too.
You'll have to
dig the bed,
bury the bulbs,
pull the weeds."
So I did my feeble part.
And God took that bulb —
burst it with life,
fed it with soil,
showered it with rain,
drew it with sunshine
Until we had a beautiful flower.
And then He seemed to say,
"Your life is like a garden
and if you'd like, we'll make it
a beautiful thing.
"I'll furnish," He said —
"the soil of grace,
the sunshine of love,
the rains of blessing,
the wonder of life
But you must do the digging."
"Lord," I said, "You just go ahead,

Make me what You want me to be;
make me a saint,
give me great faith,
fill me with compassion."
"Oh, no," He said. "You've got to
keep your heart tilled,
hoe the weeds of evil,
chop away the second-best.
I'll make you anything —
Pure,
Clean,
Noble,
Useful,
Anything
But only if you dig."

6

on making decisions

William I. Nichols, editor of *This Week Magazine,*
said that when he was a boy he used to think that
somewhere out ahead lay a magic moment when
one would be grown up and know all the answers.
Life would be easy when that point was reached.
There would be no more doubts, no uncertainties,
and in any given situation one would know exactly
what to do. Looking back over his experiences, however, he confessed, "The only thing I really learned
is that the moment of absolute certainty never
comes."

Harvard's late president, A. Lawrence, once said,
"The mark of an educated man is the ability to make
a reasoned guess on the basis of insufficient infor-

mation." Good judgment has been defined as "a good batting average in your guesses." Is it this lack of certainty that causes so many to shrink back from decision making?

Since to decide on the basis of insufficient information means to run the risk of being wrong, many look for an easier way in life. Rather than make up their minds and then act, they find it easier to procrastinate, just postpone it a while longer.

The results of this have been expressed in the words of the poet:

He was going to be all a mortal could be, tomorrow;
No one should be kinder or braver than he, tomorrow.
The greatest of workers this man would have been,
    tomorrow.
But the fact is, he died and faded from view,
And all he had left when living was through —
Was a mountain of things he intended to do, tomorrow.

This kind of thought leads to overcoming crippling dependence. The great publisher, Cyrus H. K. Curtis, was talking to his associate Edward Bok, who built the famous Bok Tower. "There are two kinds of people who never amount to much," said Mr. Curtis.

"And what are the two kinds?" asked Mr. Bok.

Mr. Curtis answered, "Those who cannot do what they are told, and those who can do nothing else."

Contrast the above philosophy of playing it safe with that expressed by Dr. M. Robins in "The Sin of Inactivity":

I'd rather be the ship that sails
And rides the billows wild and free
Than to be the ship that always fails
To leave its ports and go to sea.

I'd rather feel the sting of strife
Where gales are born and tempests roar;
Than to settle down to useless life
And rot in dry dock on the shore.

I'd rather fight some mighty wave
With honor in supreme command;
And find at last a well-earned grave,
Than die in ease upon the sand.

I'd rather drive when sea storms blow
And be the ship that always failed
To make the ports where it would go
Than be the ship that never sailed.

Some remind us of the fellow who was a victim of indecisiveness. He went to see the family psychiatrist. "So you have trouble making up your mind," said the doctor.

"Well, uh, uh," stammered the fellow, "well, uh, yes and no."

Someone once asked Mr. J. L. Kraft, the great manufacturer of cheese, to what he attributed his success. "The ability to make up my mind," replied Mr. Kraft. He went on to explain his method: "When I have a decision to make, first, I pray hard. Then I think hard, and when time is about up and I must have the answer, I say 'Lord, now you show me the next thing to do.' Then the first idea that comes into my mind after I have gone through that process is what I take to be the answer. I have been correct a large enough percentage of the time to persuade me that this course is sound."

Notice the steps in Mr. Kraft's method: (1) earnest prayer, "I pray hard"; (2) deep thought, "I think hard"; (3) faith and action, "When time is up and I must have the answer, I say, 'Lord, now you show me the next thing to do.' Then the first idea that comes to my mind . . . I take to be the answer."

Let's take those steps one at a time and examine them more closely. First, the matter of prayer. A great deal of soul-searching takes place in the senior year and after graduation. Important questions such as "Should I go to college?" "If so, where?" "Am I capable of succeeding in college?" "Should marriage come before choice of career or college?" "How will the draft affect my life?" — all these and more fill your mind.

So important are the answers to these questions! The wrong decision will seriously affect your future. How comforting in the face of these uncertainties are the words of Christ to every follower of His:

Ask and it shall be given you;
Seek, and ye shall find;
Knock, and it shall be opened unto you.
— Matthew 7:7

His will for your life can be known, at least enough of it to guide you in deciding what to do next. It is unthinkable that the Christ of Calvary could want to show us His will less than we desire to know it!

The second step was "Think hard."

Take from all your experiences whatever you think will help. Counsel with those who you think are the best qualified to help you. Consider the alternatives and the consequences of each choice.

Above all, be determined to do what you think will enable you to travel in the direction that leads to becoming more effective in the kind of service for which Christ has given you special gifts. "Ponder the path of thy feet, and let all thy ways be established" (Proverbs 4:26).

Faith and action are the third step. Now comes the "moment of truth." If we wait until *all* the answers are in, we will never be able to act. However, it is right here at the point of the mind's inability to be certain that faith makes the difference!

If this holds true, then it should follow that a strong relationship exists between faith and achievement. Evidence of this is available. A remarkable study by S. S. Visher showed that persons listed in *Who's Who in America* came from minister's families about twice as often as from families of professional men in general. A second study by Harvard and Yale, using a different criteria of eminence, showed that missionaries and sons of missionaries led the list.

Among Christian youth there is much talk about consecrating one's life to this work or that work. Decisions based on work will not be as wise as those based on faith — faith in Christ.

"A wise man's heart discerneth . . . time . . . ," wrote the inspired author of Ecclesiastes (8:5b). The importance of this time in your life calls to mind these provocative lines by Shakespeare:

> *There is a Tide in the affairs of men,*
> *Which, taken at the flood, leads on to fortune;*
> *Omitted, all the voyage of their life*
> *Is bound in shallows and in miseries.*
> — *Julius Caesar, Act IV, Scene 3*

Now the "high-tide" time for making important decisions has come and you are aware of the significance of this time." Friedrich Froebel, German educator and founder of kindergartens, points out the importance of such a time:

> *Spiritual forces when manifested in man exhibit a sequence, a succession of steps. It follows, therefore, that when a man at one period of his life has omitted to put forth his strength in a work which he knows to be in harmony with the divine order of things, there comes a time, sooner or later, when a void will be perceived; when the fruits of his omitted action ought to have appeared, and do not: they are the missing link in the chain of consequences. The measure of that void is the measure of his past inaction, and that man will never quite reach the same level of attainment that he might have touched, had he divinely energized his lost moments.*

Graduation finds you at the crossroads; you must choose which path to take — but which one?

> *Two roads diverged in the woods, and I —*
> *I took the one less travelled by.*
> *And that has made all the difference.*
> — *Robert Frost in* The Road Not Taken

The road that makes "all the difference" stretches out before you. John Oxenham, an English business-man and writer, called it the "high way" when he penned these familiar lines:

*To every man there openeth
A way, and ways, and a way
And the High Soul climbs the High Way,
And the Low Soul gropes the Low.
And in between on the misty flats
The rest drift to and fro,
But to every man there openeth
A High Way and A Low.
And every man decideth
The way his soul shall go.*

You can take the right way by listening for divine direction.

. . . Thine ears shall hear a word behind thee, saying, This is the way, walk ye in it, when ye turn to the right hand, and when ye turn to the left.
                                        — Isaiah 30:21

7

how far to turn the screw

Many years ago a young man from western Pennsylvania heard of Princeton University's president and was so deeply impressed that he decided to enroll. He took the entrance examination and failed. However, he paid President McCosh a visit before returning home.

When the president answered the door, the young man told him of his desire to enter Princeton, but that, having failed the entrance exam, he was now returning home. "But I would like to thank you," said the youth, "for what I have learned here."

President McCosh, somewhat startled, said, "Mon, what have ye learned from us?"

"How little I know," answered the youth.

"Mon, we will take ye," replied President McCosh. "Ye are two years ahead of the rest of them."

How many in your graduating class could appreciate what the famous Scottish president of Princeton had recognized in that young man? Having some knowledge of the vast difference between *what you know* and *how much there is yet to learn* will indeed mark you as a knowledgeable person.

> We have not yet arrived
> Without this growing notion:
> Our knowledge is a drop;
> Our ignorance an ocean.

Few would debate the importance of humility regarding how much we know. But we dare not stop here; we must go on to think deeply about another point contained in a story that comes from the business world.

A computer broke down and all the geniuses on the office staff tried to fix it. After their unsuccessful efforts, an expert was called in. He turned the machine on and listened to it for a few minutes. Then he took out a screw driver and turned one screw a half turn and, just like that, the machine was repaired.

When the company received a bill for $175.00 at the end of the month, the office manager went into a rage. He wrote for an itemized statement and explained exactly what the expert had done.

A few days later, the company received the itemized statement that read: "For turning one screw: 15¢; for knowing *how far* to turn the screw: $174.85."

There is no substitute for practical know-how! The person who knows "how far to turn the screw" will always find opportunities to use his knowledge and skill.

This truth needs to be spread throughout the ranks of today's "tassel movers." It is not difficult to find graduates who can talk about wanting to help mankind. The problem lies in finding idealistic youth who are willing to subject themselves to the hours and effort required for the development of excellence. Christian youth, in particular, should understand that a burden is not enough.

Can you imagine what they would do to someone who, upon entering the ward for patients about to undergo surgery, would declare while brandishing a scalpel, "I have no medical training, but I do have a burden to help suffering humanity"! When wise King Solomon began work on the magnificent temple, the call went out for workers who were highly trained and skillful: "So now send me a man skilled to work in gold, silver, bronze, and iron, and in purple, crimson, and blue fabrics, trained also in engraving, to be with skilled workers who are with me . . ." (II Chronicles 2:7).

Talent must be trained; desire must be disciplined. Life can get rough for those who don't know how far to turn the screw. As the *Living Bible* puts it, "A dull axe requires great strength; be wise and sharpen the blade" (Ecclesiastes 10:10).

What are some kinds of practical knowledge that high school graduates should consider? Perhaps we could start with the importance of vocations, since young people are bulging the labor force at a record rate of fifty thousand a week.

You don't need to be reminded that great care should be taken in choosing your work. Nobody wants to be a vocational misfit, and yet many people complain of not liking their jobs. For example, a nationwide study made by the American Institute of Public Opinion reveals that perhaps three out of every five workers are wasting their lives in jobs they hate.

How can this mistake be avoided? Some guidance regarding the problem was offered by Ruskin who said, "In order that people may be happy in their work, these three things are needed: they must be fit for it; they must not do too much of it; and they must have a sense of success in it."

Let's focus on the first thing Ruskin mentions — "they must be fit for it." This kind of analysis is not easy. Matching a person with the work for which he is best suited requires an understanding of the person as well as the work. Often young people discover interests and abilities by taking vocational tests. These tests can rate your dexterity, your ability with numbers and words and your sense of logic, insight, and judgment. Your state employment service can direct you to the proper places to take these tests. Also, you can take such tests at most colleges and universities.

Another kind of knowledge of great value highlights job trends for those who will be entering the world of work immediately after graduation. You have graduated from high school at a time when the need for technical workers is becoming critical. Openings in this area include data-processing specialists, electronics technicians, technical secretaries, lab assistants, draftsmen, supervisors of production control, technical photographers, government safety inspectors.

Authorities predict an annual shortage of nearly half a million skilled craftsmen: carpenters, bricklayers, plumbers, electricians, mechanics, lathe operators, machinists.

A strong demand will exist for sales and office workers: typists, secretaries, stenographers, telephone operators, office clerks, retail and wholesale salesmen.

Other openings will be available for service workers: cooks, waitresses, policemen, firemen, hair stylists.

When the time comes to seek employment it helps to be aware of some common-sense things about the interview. Personnel directors responsible for interviewing young people who are looking for jobs seem to agree on basic points. Their advice stresses the following and is worth careful consideration:

1. Develop the fundamental skills of reading, writing, and arithmetic. One company on the West Coast found that four out of every ten high school graduates were unable "to demonstrate an ability to learn the rudiments of even a relatively simple work assignment."

2. *Dress appropriately when you go job hunting.* The "take me for what I am, not for how I look" attitude won't persuade prospective employers to change their policy to suit the applicant. Fashion experts say we dress the way we think and we act the way we dress. Behavioral scientists have found that character correlates with cleanliness and appropriate styles of dress.

3. *Show common courtesy.* One personnel director of a large company who interviews dozens of young people every day complained of youthful applicants who cracked gum and blew smoke in his face!

4. *Go to the interview by yourself.* Leave the boyfriend, girlfriend, or relative at home

5. *Display the "I really want to work" attitude.*

6. *Understand the principle of first things first.* You don't need to ask about a pension plan in the first interview.

7. *Answer all questions on the application.* If you can't respond to a question put a dash beside it so the personnel director will know you didn't overlook it.

8. *Be on time.* Punctuality reflects consideration for the personnel director, and shows that you are a person with a sense of responsibility.

9. *Write or print legibly.* Carelessness in this matter wastes the personnel director's time.

10. *Remember to trust Christ to help you.* He knows the anxieties of young job hunters. Having a sense of His presence will steady you and give an assurance of His guiding presence.

A third good thing to keep in mind is that the selection of workers for the best jobs has become highly specialized. Employers are now advised by psychologists to look for certain characteristics in prospective employees. Dr. George W. Crane, a psychologist, tells employers that if they have a choice they should know that:

Churchgoers are more efficient than nonchurch attenders.
Drinkers are less efficient than those who stay away from alcoholic beverages.
Smokers tend to be less efficient than nonsmokers.
The person who takes extra courses or studies on his own time is preferable to the one who does not.
The person whose credit rating is good is a better worker than the one who can't manage his money.
The one who organizes his equipment and tools and puts them away is a better worker than the one who doesn't.

According to an ancient Persian proverb:

He who knows not, and knows not that he knows not,
Is a fool,
    Shun him;
He who knows not, and knows that he knows not,
Is a child,
    Teach him;
He who knows and knows not that he knows,
Is asleep,
    Wake him;
He who knows, and knows that he knows,
Is wise,
    Follow him.

Now link the last sentence with this statement by Jesus Christ: "I am the truth . . ." (John 14:6). Startling, isn't it? For not only does it mean that Christ knew and knew that He knew. It also means that He boldly claimed that all knowledge based on truth has its source in *Him*. This discovery came to a nineteen-year-old coed who said to me: "Every subject I take — psychology, English, history, or Bible — leads to Christ and reveals more of Him."

A clear relationship exists between knowing "how far to turn the screw" and knowing the Source of all knowledge. Read about the education of a youth named Daniel and his friends in the first chapter of the Book of Daniel. There you will find that because they lived godly lives, "God gave them knowledge and skill in all learning and wisdom" (1:17).

If you have caught the idea that your work is the vocational expression of *you in cooperation with divine purpose,* you are one of the privileged of your generation. This idea elevates and dignifies whatever work you do, and motivates you toward excellence. Further, this idea was held by Christ, as Dr. Leslie Weatherhead so beautifully writes:

> *See the young man Christ! On the hilltop at night looking into the face of God, the realization of his divine purpose flooding his mind and enflaming his emotions. Then follow him early next morning to his carpenter shop. Watch as he sharpens his tools and lays out plans, throttling down his possibilities to that cottage home and carpenter shop. He is not irked, not resentful. And for 20 years, he faithfully stays with the task.*

A concern for the practical is essentially a *Christian* concern as the poet demonstrates:

> *. . . he walked the self-same road,*
> *And he bore the self-same load,*
> *When the carpenter of Nazareth*
> *Made common things for God.*

8

you can't take it
by correspondence

A father and his small son were looking the toy department over when the boy's attention was attracted to a strange-looking toy. "What kind of toy is this?" asked the father.

The salesman explained, "It's a toy designed to prepare children for the space age."

"How does it do that?"

"You see all these pieces? No matter how you try to put them together, the toy won't work!"

Of course, there is such a thing as exaggerating a point, and the poet of the following expressed it well:

Some folks worry and sputter
And push and shove,
Hunting little molehills
To make mountains of.

However, a brief look at your world will hardly allow you to be guilty of mistaking what seems ahead as "molehills." What does your generation face?

1. Increased mechanization of life, characterized by great scientific and technological advancement. Automation has become an established part of our way of life. Some fear that man-versus-machine contests are becoming more and more a one-sided affair. Witness the set of computers that are supplementing the fatherly role of advising Sammy where to go to college. The memory cores of these computers are filled with facts and figures on almost three thousand U.S. colleges. Aided by their guidance counselors, students fill out questionnaires, giving their ability to pay, their preferences and their motives. This information is fed to the computer. Out comes a complete roster of possible colleges!

Computerization and automation are here to stay, but not without their effect on man. One of their effects may be illustrated by the story of the two cows grazing along the roadside. A large milk truck passes by. On the side of the truck are painted in bold strokes these words: Pasteurized, Homogenized, Vitamin B Added. After watching the truck go by, one cow looks at the other and says, "Makes you feel kinda inadequate, doesn't it?"

Yet, a refreshing bit of news came from the University of Maryland recently. It seems that a computer flunked arithmetic! Academc vice-president Hornbake explained that the failure was due to an error in programming. This caused the computer to issue incorrect grade averages for several hundred students!

2. Racial strife. The social, economic, and psychological relationships between races are changing. The colored people of the world constitute about three-fourths of the world's population. The time has passed when a man's skin color carries built-in advantages and disadvantages. Performance, not pedigree, is what matters now. Yours is the generation that can achieve "liberty and justice for all."

3. Population explosion and food shortage. The earth's population doubled in the last ninety years ending in 1950, when it reached an estimated 2.5 billion. Predictions are that it will double again in less than half that time.

While the world's population is growing at the rate of 2 percent per year, the world's food supplies are growing at the rate of only 1 percent per year. We used to hear this familiar sentence: "Half of all the world's children will go to bed hungry tonight." Now it goes like this: "Seventy percent of the world's children will go to sleep hungry tonight."

Eminent scientists forecast famine by 1980 in Africa, Asia and Latin America. Dr. Raymond Ewell, vice-president of research at State University of New

York at Buffalo, says this threat of famine is "the greatest and most nearly insoluble problem in the history of the world."

4. Lawlessness. Even though government officials are concerned with the magnitude of the staggering crime rate today, the problem of stemming the tide seems almost insurmountable. Muggings on the streets of our larger cities have become almost commonplace. Large numbers of our population are afraid to walk on the streets at night in their own neighborhoods. Shoplifting has become one of the major headaches of retailers everywhere. Organized crime has become firmly entrenched. One has only to glance at his daily newspaper to recognize the severity of the crime problem.

Especially disturbing is the phenomenal increase in crimes committed by young people in their early and late teens. Fifteen- and sixteen-year-olds have the highest arrest rate in the Country. Serious crime among youth is said to be increasing nearly four times as fast as the youth population. Juvenile courts are hardpressed to keep up with the work load thrust upon them.

5. World-wide unrest, communist aggression, threat of thermonuclear war and interplanetary problems.

All this makes the picture anything but appealing. It reminds one of the London policeman who, while walking his beat on the Waterloo bridge, spied a man about to jump. The bobby (London police are called *bobbies*) managed to get to him just in time. "Come now," said the bobby. "Tell me what is the matter. Is it money?"

The man shook his head.

"Is it your wife?"

Again a negative reply.

"Well, what is it then?" persisted the bobby.

"I'm worried about the condition of the world," admitted the man.

"Oh, come now," replied the bobby, reassuringly. "It couldn't be as bad as all that. Walk up and down the bridge with me and let's talk it over."

And so the two men walked along discussing the world's problems for about an hour and then they *both* jumped over!

More important than the conditions themselves, however, is the way in which they are interpreted by the individual. A great psychiatrist has said, "Attitudes are more important than facts." Another way of putting it is that we see things not as *they* are, but as *we* are.

What about the way *your* generation sees things? Great amounts of costly research have attempted to explain the mystique of modern youth. Virginia Satir, the family therapist, says, "This generation is made up of searchers." Searching for what? Perhaps the answer is partly found in the word *identity*. As one thoughtful young person stated, "I value the building of myself." One young man when asked what he feared most replied, "Getting lost in a maze of IBM cards in a file, molded; pushed from what I am into what everybody else is."

Some studies of youth have uncovered a noticeable lack of spirit of adventure. This lack of ambition seems to be linked with an excessive concern for security. Only one in fifty of the youth polled in one study wanted to become a minister or social worker. A coed may have revealed the key to the problem by stating, "All we need is a motive; then you'll see."

When a person faces problems that look unsolvable, problems over which he has little control or for which he has little responsibility, might he not cover his fear and resentment with "coolness" or negativism to life? Is it not possible for a culture to become so shallow in its social and spiritual relationships, goals and values that it might create in the young an inordinate urge for "kicks"? Not a few responsible adults are asking, "Can we expect true commitment on the part of youth when their adult examples demonstrate indifference to crucial issues and carelessness regarding the ordering of their own lives? And might not youth become overly concerned with themselves when adults, instead of using their maturity and experience to guide and support the young, demonstrate an inability to age gracefully — even to the point of taking on youth's fashion style, ways and style of life?"

Is the picture all gloom and no gleam? A young lady who was valedictorian of her senior class realized that each individual must answer for himself.

She began her valedictory address to more than four hundred fellow graduates like this:

"Tonight as we stand ready to take our first step down life's pathway, I will ask one question: What will our lives be — a farce or a force?"

An interesting question! She took the definitions of the words *farce* and *force* from Webster:

> *Farce: A ridiculous or empty show, something to be laughed at, perhaps ridiculed.*
> *Force: Something that possesses great strength and which has a great effect on that with which it comes in contact.*

The rest of the address developed the idea that whether one becomes a force or a farce depends upon the way he relates to the world. The farce may have impressive intentions, but when faced with difficulty and temptation he gives up the fight. He reminds you of the young man who lived back in the days when Joe Louis was heavyweight champion of the world. In those days many boys dreamed of becoming boxers. Most of them had no idea of the rugged training necessary to learning the manly art. This particular lad approached a boxing teacher who gave private lessons. He was informed by this teacher that before anybody could box for pay, he had to take a course consisting of twenty lessons.

The student agreed to the arrangement and his first lesson began. He was shown a film on boxing and heard a brief lecture. Then the teacher took the student to another room where they dressed for the ring. They climbed through the ropes and the match was on. Having been a tough, successful fighter, the teacher proceeded to knock his student down three times. By the time the practice was over, the student's face was bruised, cut and swollen. The teacher instructed the student to go to the shower and clean himself up, and come back by the office for the second lesson's assignment. While he showered the battered youth was thinking seriously about those nineteen remaining lessons.

When he returned to the office, the student asked his teacher, "You say there are twenty lessons in this course?"

"That's right," answered the teacher.

"And I just took one today?"

"Right again."

"And I have to finish the other nineteen before I can get money for boxing?"

"That was the agreement."

Scratching his head and shifting his stance, the student looked at his teacher quizzically and said, "Well, sir, I wonder if I could take the other nineteen lessons by correspondence?"

The farce would have the same inclination; he would like to take the rugged courses in life by correspondence!

But not so the force. He is the person who is not afraid to risk making mistakes, even failure. These turbulent times may chill the farce but they will challenge the force! Opportunity opens its doors to members of your generation. Here and there are heard youthful voices that promise an acceptance of the challenge. One girl hopes: "I'll be elected senator from Oregon. I want to stick pins under people." Carl Sandburg's request may be shared by more of your generation than some think. He wrote:

> Lay me on an Anvil, O God.
> Beat me and hammer me into a crowbar.
> Let me pry loose old walls,
> Let me lift and loosen old foundations!

This sounds like New Testament language. Dr. J. Wallace Hamilton reminds us:

> We who hold this Bible in our hands, we who are followers of the way of Christ are part of the oldest and most radical revolution in human history. It is so old that some of us have forgotten how radical it is, so misshapen that some people are actually shocked to be told that Jesus was a rebel, a revolutionist. So long have they accepted the false picture of a gentle Jesus, meek and mild, that they have forgotten the central fact of our faith: He was executed as an insurrectionist, regarded as an agitator too dangerous to live, and was put to death as a public menace: in His heart was a deep protest against the evils that blight man, and in His mind was a great, thought-out plan for man's salvation.

Compare the Christ with any great person in history and you will recognize Him to be the greatest "foundation loosener and lifter" of them all. And as you plan for the future in this uncertain and rapidly changing age, He is able to offer unequaled opportunity for you to make a meaningful contribution to your world.

Years ago when I first began to teach teen-agers in the Houston Public Schools, I would pen a favorite verse in annuals, books, etc, for high school graduates. I would like to share with you the one that has come to mean the most to me in these turbulent times:

> *Trust in the Lord with all thine heart;*
>   *and lean not unto thine own understanding.*
> *In all thy ways acknowledge Him,*
>   *and He shall direct thy paths.*
>
> — *Proverbs 3:5, 6*

9

questions and answers

Following are some of the questions most commonly asked by high school graduates. Of course space has limited the scope and content but perhaps you will find some of the answers helpful.

Q. What kind of specific advice regarding how to become a success can be given?

A. Let William James give this counsel: "Let no youth have any anxiety about the upshot of his education, whatever the line of it may be. If he keep faithfully busy each hour of the working day, he may safely leave the final result to itself. He can with perfect certainty count on waking up some fine morning to find himself one of the competent ones of his generation, in whatever pursuit he may have singled out. Silently, between all the details of his business, the *power of judging* in all that class of matter will have built itself up within him as a possession that will never pass away. Young people should know this truth in advance. The ignorance of it has probably engendered more discouragement and faint-heartedness in youths embarking on arduous careers than all other causes put together."

Now the Scriptures: "Constantly remind the people about these laws, and you yourself must think about them every day and every night so that you will be sure to obey all of them. For only then will you succeed" (Joshua 1:8, *The Living Bible*).

Q. I'm trying to decide whether or not to go to college. What kinds of information do I need to help me make this decision?

A. You probably know that nationally speaking, about the same number of high school graduates go to college as don't go.

When freshmen are asked for reasons why they decided to go to college they typically give the following answers:

To get a better job.

To acquire a general education.

To earn more money.

To please parents.

To get away from parents.

To meet interesting people.

To have something to do.

Of the number of young people entering college

roughly half of them will drop out before graduation. Many studies have been made to determine why the drop-out rate is so high. Among the findings that the researchers consistently discover is that of knowledge of a life purpose as it relates to education. Most youth who drop out of college possess enough mental ability to succeed as college students. However, if they cannot relate their subjects and classroom work to present needs and future goals, then the academic road becomes too rough and leads to no desired destination.

Those who *do* travel the academic road to graduation often speak of experiencing greater personal growth, a sharper sense of purpose, and a higher development of skills. Any college worthy of the name should offer each student the opportunities to discover and develop his abilities so that he can use himself at increasingly higher levels of performance to the glory of God.

Two false views of college need to be examined. One view sees going to college as the big cop-out. Those who hold this attitude give reasons that might be classified three ways: 1) Lack of personal freedom: "I don't want to relinquish my personal rights." They chide their friends for going to college just to get parental approval or because most of their friends are going. 2) Lack of purpose: "I'm going because there is nothing better to do." 3) Lack of sense of involvement: "I'm going to escape for awhile."

The idea of college being a cop-out seems to be rooted in a belief that instead of contributing to growth, college stifles it. This idea should not be totally rejected, for not all colleges do provide the kind of stimulation and environment that is conducive to personal development. Neither, however, should this idea go unchallenged. Those who hold it seem to be unable to offer convincing evidence that *their* lifestyle offers much that deserves to be widely imitated.

The second false view that many who enroll in college seem to have is that college is the royal route to success. They think, "College will convert me into all I should be." They view college as a cure-all, a guarantee of a secure future.

These false expectations of college are a major reason for dropping out. Every incoming freshman should know that college should provide the proper environment and opportunities, but the outcome depends on the responses the student makes.

Q. How can I get information on Bible Colleges?

A. Christian graduates are being strongly attracted to Bible Colleges. Among the advantages they find are a rich spiritual environment, high academic standards, highly qualified professors and opportunities for meaningful service. For more information write:

Accrediting Association of Bible Colleges
Office of the Executive Director
Box 543
Wheaton, Illinois

Q. My parents cannot afford to send me to college. How can I finance my own education?

A. Loan programs are available. Contact your state department of education and your high school or college counselor for information. Be sure to consider banks, college loan companies, foundations and other loan agencies. Your father might inquire at his company about college financial aid programs of assistance to students.

According to an estimate by the U.S. Office of Education as many as 1.18 million American college students (roughly one out of every six undergraduate college students) are receiving some governmental aid in financing their educations. Why not see if you can qualify for government aid under the National Defense Education Act (NDEA), Economic Opportunity Act (EOA), the low-cost (3 percent) long term loans to students by commercial lending institutions?

Scholarships may be available to you. Check with your school or community library to acquaint yourself with the commercially published scholarship guides. Physically handicapped and children of servicemen killed or permanently disabled in action may obtain benefit grants and other special financial aid.

The college of your choice probably has an employment service. If the college is located in a large city, employment may not be too difficult to find, but be sure to remember that school comes first!

In his book *Prayer Changes Things,* Dr. Charles L. Allen tells about a remarkable minister friend. As a six-year-old boy, Dr. Allen's friend was accidentally shot by an older brother. The bullet shot away several fingers of his right hand and permanently impaired the elbow of the other arm.

Time passed and finally the boy graduated from high school. He wanted to go to college but realized that his parents were financially unable to help him. He bought a second-hand typewriter and learned to type. Working as a part-time secretary, he paid for his college education.

Then he went to Yale to obtain a Ph.D. degree. To finance his education there, he worked in the cafeteria and at night read proof in a newspaper office from 11 o'clock until 4 o'clock in the morning. His doctoral dissertation was a study of ninth-century manuscripts written in Vulgate Latin, a language he didn't know. He not only had to learn Vulgate Latin, but before his research could be completed, he had to learn six other languages: Greek, Hebrew, German, French, Aramaic, and Syrian. Not only did he get his Ph.D.; he also made an important contribution to Biblical knowledge.

When Dr. Allen asked his friend how he managed to overcome his handicaps, he replied, "We all have limitations of some kind and we all have abilities. I thought about what I could do and never worried about anything else. Our limitations can be either stepping stones or stumbling blocks."

Q. How important is higher education to girls?

A. It is not unusual even in today's world to come in contact with those who feel that there is no need for girls to continue their schooling beyond high school. Their reasoning is usually based upon the idea that after marriage they will be at home with their families, and who needs higher education to be a homemaker?

Those who argue that higher education is important only for men who must "work" for a living forget one important aspect of the question. Lydia H. Sigourney, an immensely popular author of the middle 1880s, touched upon this facet of education when, in *Letters to Young Ladies* (1851), she asked:

> *Is it not important that the sex to whom nature has entrusted the molding of the whole mass of mind in its first foundation should be acquainted with the structure and developments of mind?*

Developing this idea, she continued,

> *Admitting, then, that whether she wills it or not, whether she even knows it or not, she is still a teacher. . . .*
>
> *Of what unspeakable importance, then, is her education, who gives lessons before any other instructor; who preoccupies the unwritten page of being; who produces impressions which only death can obliterate; and mingles with the candle-dream what shall be recorded in eternity.*
>
> *And now, Guardians of Education . . . Parents . . . you have so generously lavished on woman the means of knowledge — complete your education by urging her to gather its treasures with a tireless hand. Demand of her as a debt the highest excellence she is*

capable of attaining. Summon her to abandon selfish motives and inglorious ease. Incite her to those virtues which promote the permanence and health of nations. Make her accountable for the character of the next generation. Give her solemn charge in the presence of men and of angels. Gird her with the whole armour of education and piety, and see if she be not faithful to her children, to her country, and to her God.

Mrs. Lyndon B. Johnson expressed the same sentiment when she said, "When you teach a man, you teach an individual. But when you teach a woman, you teach a family."

Q. What is the number one consideration for admittance to college?

A. To get the answer, the Educational Records Bureau of New York City secured the following information from 560 questionnaires:

1. High school grade record.
2. Recommendation of the school principal or or counselor.
3. College Board Scholastic Aptitude Test (SAT).
4. Applicant's class standing.

Personal qualities count more with colleges now than they did ten years ago. Nine out of ten colleges want to know about the student's character, his emotional stability, attitudes and leadership qualities. Results of personal interviews are included in admission decisions by 80 percent of the colleges.

This indicates that a student's personal character is an important criterion; good scholarship is to be desired but it is the student's *total* record that colleges evaluate.

Q. What is a college education worth?

A. Approximately $444,000 in monetary value. Every year in college is worth a minimum of $35,000. These figures were compiled by David G. Funk, an economist for John Hancock Life Insurance Company. The economist estimated that for every dollar invested on a college education, the student gets perhaps $20 in return.

Another point to consider was given by Mr. Willard Wirtz, Secretary of Labor: "Any high school senior in doubt about whether to seek a higher education finds an unflattering proposition: the machine now has a high school education, in the sense that it can do most jobs that a high school graduate can do. So machines will get the jobs, because they work for less than a living wage. A person needs fourteen years of education to compete with machines."

Dr. L. H. Adolfson, of the University of Wisconsin, tells a story that contains excellent guidance for those who wonder if they should have more education. The story is about three horsemen of ancient times who were riding across a desert. As they crossed the dry bed of a river, out of the darkness a voice called, "Halt."

They obeyed. They were told to dismount, pick up a handful of pebbles, put the pebbles in their pockets and remount.

After they had done as they were instructed, the voice said, "You have done as I commanded. Tomorrow at sun-up you will be both glad and sorry." The three horsemen rode away thinking about the strange prediction.

The next morning at sunrise, they reached into their pockets and found that a miracle had happened. Instead of pebbles, they pulled out diamonds, rubies, and other precious stones. Then they saw the truth of the prophecy. They were both glad and sorry — glad they had taken some, and sorry they had not taken more. . . .

And this, points out Dr. Adolfson, is the story of education.

Q. I am thinking about getting married, but am also considering entering college. How would continuing my education affect my chances for future marital success?

A. Very favorably, according to most studies on the subject. Chances for marital success increase with the amount of education acquired by both husband and wife. Higher education will increase your ability as a parent, too.

Keep in mind that a few years in college add greatly to your maturity. This means your choice of a marriage mate will be made on the basis of a more mature judgment because of your having developed an "educated" perspective.

Q. Can an average ("C") student succeed in college?

A. High school graduates with a "C" average should not conclude that they are not "smart" enough to succeed in college. Of course, some colleges and universities are highly selective and competition is exceptionally difficult. Average students are accepted by many good colleges and universities. Don't overlook the junior college, for it can serve as an ideal training ground for both testing your ability to succeed in college and providing you with greater personal attention from your professor. Many junior colleges offer vocational programs that help you develop "marketable skills" suitable to your style of life and community opportunities.

Average students who possess strong ambition, determination and a willingness to work hard can succeed in college. Sometimes "C" students in high school become superior students in college!

Q. I'm having trouble getting accepted for college. What should I do?

A. Apply through one of these nonprofit admission centers:

College Admissions Assistance Center
461 Park Avenue South
New York, New York 10016

College Admissions Center
801 Davis Street
Evanston, Illinois 60201

Council for Advancement of Small Colleges
1327 18th Street N.W.
Washington, D.C. 20036

(For $1.00 you can obtain a directory of colleges which are "unaccredited," but whose courses are given full credit at certain recognized institutions if you want to transfer later on.)

Q. After I decide upon a college, then what?

A. 1. Obtain a catalog of the college or university you want to attend: You will be able to get it from the admissions officer at the college or in a library. Also obtain the catalog of the college of your second choice.

2. Use the catalog to find out if you will be able to meet the academic standards required for admission.

3. Select two or three specific courses you think you might like to take and for which you will be able to meet the requirements. Do not make a final decision too hastily.

4. Note all dates with respect to enrollment, entrance and scholarship examinations so that you will be able to complete all forms on time.

5. Make a budget for your first college year as follows:

a. For tuition (see college catalog) $
b. For residence, if any (see
                        catalog) $
c. Miscellaneous college expenses
                  (see catalog) $
d. Books (minimum $50) $
e. Spending money, $ a week
         times   30 weeks equals $
f. Caution money for emergencies
              (at least $50) $
g. Transportation costs $
h. Clothes ($100 to $250 is average) $
i. Other items, such as possible
   medical and dental expenses,
   Christmas presents, etc. $

                        TOTAL $_____

Q. If going to college is presently out of the question, how can I further my education?

A. Correspondence courses are available. Many of these courses can be taken for college credit. For information include fifty cents and write "Guide to Correspondence Study," National University Extension Association, University of Minnesota, Minneapolis, Minnesota 55404. More information can be obtained free by ordering the "Directory of Accredited Private Home Study Schools" from National Home Study Council, 1601 18th Street, Washington, D.C. 20009.

Q. I've had my fill of school and formal education. I'd like to do something with my hands. Where can I get information on job opportunities that offer training programs and apprenticeships?

A. Contact the local branch office of your State Employment Security Commission to set up an appointment for aptitude testing and/or vocational counseling. That office will also have a listing of various job opportunities and apprenticeship programs available in your area of interest.

Employers in your city probably have an association which keeps an up-to-date listing of openings, along with job descriptions and on-the-job training opportunities.

National firms, such as General Motors, offer excellent trainee programs, including aptitude testing and apprenticeships in a wide variety of jobs.

Q. What about patriotism?

A. Our nation's awareness of youth eighteen to twenty-one years of age recently found expression in the Twenty-sixth Amendment to the Constitution. The nation-wide effort to lower the voting age to eighteen ended June 30, 1971, when Ohio became the thirty-eighth state to ratify the Amendment. This allowed eleven million young Americans to exercise the highest political privilege, that of casting their own vote. It is a privilege overdue and you can show that you can handle it by your responsible involvement in party politics, social causes, and government.

In these days demanding honor, strength and devotion to God and country, the following words ring true:

On our side there is nothing but the light. That is why the victory will be with us. For to enlighten is to deliver. Every increase in liberty involves increased responsibility. Nothing is graver than freedom; liberty has burdens of her own, and lays on the conscience all the chains which she unshackles from the limbs. Let us therefore take heed to what we are doing; we live in a difficult time and are answerable at once to the past and to the future.

from Deeds and Words *by Victor Hugo*

Q. What are the alternatives for high school graduates who are seeking to live meaningful, productive lives, but who do not plan to go to college?

A. 1. Practical training is necessary to start a career. This "vocational" training is offered by occupational schools and community colleges. Check your public library for a copy of *The Occupational Outlook Handbook* for information on (1) kinds of jobs available, (2) where various kinds of work are performed, (3) what qualifications and training are needed, (4) salaries and working conditions, (5) obtainability of various jobs in the future, and (6) where further information is available.

2. Apprenticeship in a trade may be the route to a satisfying job. As an apprentice you would have a full-time job while you learn the skills of your trade. For more information, write the U.S. Bureau of Apprenticeship and Training, Patrick Henry Building, 601 D Street N.W., Washington, DC 20004.

3. Military service with its advantages and disadvantages is another alternative.

4. Other options include volunteer service, a year of traveling (if you have the finances!), and working to make money for some occupational training effort in the future.

You are fortunate to live in a nation that provides its young people with many ways to find personal fulfillment. With God's guidance you can find training and work that are suited to your abilities and interests. And there never has been a time in the history of our country when Christian youth were more needed in every area of its professional-vocational life.

10

go claim your mountain

A certain high school class toured the White House. After they returned to class, their teacher asked them to write their impressions of the visit. One boy penned this brief but revealing statement: "I was glad to have this opportunity to visit my future home."

William James, the famous psychologist, would have predicted great things for the lad! James was convinced that "our belief at the beginning of a doubtful undertaking is the one thing that assures the successful outcome of any venture."

One of the most inspiring examples of this is found in the fourteenth chapter of Joshua. A great scene is described. Having crossed over the River Jordan into Canaan, the Israelites now await their inheritance. Joshua, their great leader, stands before them and gives to each respective tribe its inheritance, according to the Lord's command to Moses.

Then an individual breaks rank and strides confidently toward Joshua. The two men meet and stand in full sight of the great multitude. Everyone recognizes the other man as Caleb, whose heroics were known to every family.

Caleb had come with a claim to make. He had been living with a dream for a long time. Now that dream was about to come true. He reminds Joshua of the time when they both were much younger. They and ten other men had been chosen as representatives of each of their tribes to spy out the land of Canaan. Upon their return only Joshua and Caleb believed it was possible for their people to possess the land that "flowed with milk and honey," the land that God had promised the Jewish nation.

Because of the way they exercised their faith, the two men were greatly blessed by God. Joshua became Moses' successor and Caleb, a trusted and courageous soldier and leader.

But somehow, Caleb kept remembering a beautiful place he had seen while spying out the land. The place was called Hebron. "One day," he often thought to himself, "I'll have Hebron for my own."

The day had come. At last the great moment was here and Caleb speaks: ". . . I am as strong this day as I was in the day that Moses sent me: as my strength was then, even so is my strength now . . .

Now therefore give me this mountain. . . ." What confidence! What a claim!

Caleb's belief in his ability to accomplish things needs to be shared by every high school graduate. The following anonymous poem tells why:

> If you think you are beaten, you are,
>   If you think you dare not, you don't
> If you'd like to win, but you think you can't,
>   It's almost a cinch you won't.
>
> If you think you'll lose, you're lost,
>   For out in the world we find
> Success begins with a fellow's will,
>   It's all in the state of mind.
>
> If you think you're outclassed, you are,
>   You've got to think high to rise,
> You've got to be sure of yourself before
>   You can ever win a prize.
>
> Life's battle doesn't always go
>   To the swifter or faster man,
> But sooner or later the man who wins
>   Is the man "who thinks he can."

". . . All things are possible to him that believeth," said Jesus (Mark 9:23). Is this just good reading, or does it really work? Those who have tried it have

> subdued kingdoms
>   wrought righteousness
>   obtained promises
>   stopped the mouths of lions
>   quenched the violence of fire
>   escaped the edge of the sword
>   out of weakness were made strong
>   waxed valiant in fight
>   — Hebrews 11:33, 34

91

Let enough of this get inside you and like Paul you, too, will be saying, "I can do all things through Christ which strengtheneth me" (Philippians 4:13).

Now this quality of confidence has to be *learned.* Those who have a mountain they want to claim must struggle with doubt, failure, and discouragement.

In a certain classroom at Exeter, New Hampshire, a youth was asked to give an oral report to his classmates. Each attempt ended in a humiliating failure. Recalling his experience he confessed: "I could not speak before the school. Many a piece did I commit to memory, and recite and rehearse in my own room, over and over again, and yet, when the day came, when my name was called, and all eyes turned to my seat, I could not raise myself from it. When the occasion was over, I went home and wept bitter tears of mortification." Later the youth decided that he would conquer his timidity if it killed him. Did he succeed? To know his name is to have the answer — Daniel Webster, still acclaimed by many as the greatest orator in American history.

Caleb's extraordinary confidence led to an extraordinary conquest. Doesn't it always? It so happened that Hebron was the most heavily fortified area in all of Canaan. Three great giants and their people had been successful in defeating all would-be conquerors — until Caleb came along!

Caleb was given divine help because he "wholly followed the Lord." So will you! Of all the tribes given inheritances, only Caleb's completely conquered the enemy. He was not going to live with "what might have been." His claim was great; his confidence unfailing; his conquest complete. The next-to-the-last verse of the fourteenth chapter of Joshua gives the thrilling result of Caleb's inspiring faith: "Hebron therefore became the inheritance of Caleb . . . unto this day, because he wholly followed the Lord . . . ."

How about *your* "Hebron"? You, too, can claim your mountain! These can be yours: a radiant Christian influence, highly developed talents, high ideals, a well-furnished mind, singleness of purpose, a cultured, Christlike personality, unfailing tact, deep understanding and compassion, and above all, eternal life.

Great mountains, these! No wonder the poet pleads:

> *Bring me men to match my mountains,*
> *Bring me men to match my plains;*
> *Men with empires in their purpose,*
> *And new eras in their brains.*
> — *Sam Walter Foss*

In these days of "fun fests," "sit-ins," "love-ins," "turn-ons," "tune-ins," and "drop-outs," the passion is for pleasure, the quest is for convenience, and the search is for security. But the mountains are available only to the men.

There is a divine purpose for your life. Out there somewhere is your Hebron. As you look at it think about these stirring words from the great Phillips Brooks: "Oh, do not pray for easy lives. Pray to be strong men and women. Do not pray for tasks equal to your powers. Pray for powers equal to your tasks. Then the doing of your work will be no miracle; but you shall be a miracle. Every day you shall wonder at yourself, at the richness of life which has come to you by the grace of God."

Consider your resources. You have infinite power behind you, Christ's abiding presence within you, and divine purpose guiding you. Your tassel has been moved and you are on your way. Consider this counsel from Martin Luther, the great reformer, who exclaimed, "Oh! how great and glorious a thing it is to have before one the Word of God! With that we may at all times feel joyous and secure; we need never be in want of consolation, for we see before us, in all its brightness, the pure and right way."

Everything you need for successful mountain-claiming has been provided. You have moved the tassel and your "Hebron" awaits your claim. Remember as you begin your journey that ". . . all things work together for good to them that love God, to them who are the called according to his purpose. What shall we then say to these things? If God be for us who can be against us? He that spared not his own Son, but delivered him up for us all, how shall he not with him also freely give us *all things?"* (Romans 8:28, 31, 32).